C000220699

Renita Boyle has been described as 'a ball of imagination and inventivenes spellbound and older listeners thinking. She features regularly in a variety of settings and is as passionate about training as telling. She is listed in the Scottish Storytelling Directory and the Scottish Book trust. Her published work includes Parable Fun for Little Ones *(Barnabas, 2007) and* The Storytime Bible *(Barnabas, 2011). Renita is married to Eric, the minister of Kirkcowan and Wigtown parish churches. They have one son, Jude, and live in Wigtown, Scotland's national book town, which is famed for its annual book festival.*

You can contact Renita at http://renitaboyle.com.

Barnabas for Children® is a registered word mark and the logo is a registered device mark of The Bible Reading Fellowhip.

Text copyright © Renita Boyle 2011
The author asserts the moral right
to be identified as the author of this work

Published by
The Bible Reading Fellowship
15 The Chambers, Vineyard
Abingdon OX14 3FE
United Kingdom
Tel: +44 (0)1865 319700
Email: enquiries@brf.org.uk
Website: www.brf.org.uk
BRF is a Registered Charity

ISBN 978 1 84101 702 0

First published 2011
10 9 8 7 6 5 4 3 2 1 0
All rights reserved

Acknowledgments
Unless otherwise stated, scripture quotations are taken from the Contemporary English Version of the Bible published by HarperCollins Publishers, copyright © 1991, 1992, 1995 American Bible Society.

Scripture quotations taken from the Holy Bible, New International Version, copyright © 1973, 1978, 1984, 1995 by International Bible Society, are used by permission of Hodder & Stoughton Publishers, a member of the Hachette Livre UK Group. All rights reserved. 'NIV' is a registered trademark of International Bible Society. UK trademark number 1448790.

Scripture quotations from THE MESSAGE. Copyright © by Eugene H. Peterson 1993, 1994, 1995. Used by permission of NavPress Publishing.

Scripture quotations marked (NLT) are taken from the Holy Bible, New Living Translation, copyright © 1996, 2004. Used by permission of Tyndale House Publishers, Inc., Wheaton, Illinois 60189. All rights reserved.

A catalogue record for this book is available from the British Library

Printed in Singapore by Craft Print International Ltd

Parachute Fun
for everyone

Renita Boyle

**50 playchute activities
for telling Bible stories,
teaching and
worship**

Acknowledgments

The use of playchutes (parachutes designed for play) in ministry is well established but less well developed. This resource aims to provide something new as well as a fresh approach to the tried and true. Indeed, many of the activities here adapt or incorporate popular games that may be familiar to you. It would be impossible to credit any one source for these as they are, by definition, widely known and available. However, those that I have found most useful are listed in the resources section on page 127.

I would particularly like to thank SeamStress Ltd, who have compiled a comprehensive collection of general playchute games and advice from experienced users. I am particularly grateful for their practical advice on safe play. Among their booklets is Playchutes in Christian Teaching: Colour and Number Dice Games for Christian Ministry. *It includes a variety of activities that use colour/number symbolism and large inflatable dice.*

Jan Dyer's 100 Children's Club Activities *is also excellent. It includes some chute-telling ideas for the life of Jesus, the Christian life and the New Testament lake stories. It also offers good general advice on running a club and a variety of simple and effective storytelling methods.*

I also appreciated Duncan Dyason's downloadable booklet of general playchute games, complete with full colour photos.

Finally, I would like to thank all of those who have supported me in the writing of this resource: Eric for his devotion, Jude for his delightfulness; the Bestels, Dunns and Robinsons for their unending encouragement, enthusiasm and energy; the Harts for their prayers; Helen, Diane and Kriss for their friendship. I would also like to thank the kids from the Junction and the many others who have piloted these ideas for me, having great fun in the process.

Photocopy permission

The right to photocopy material in *Parachute Fun for Everyone* is granted for the pages that contain the photocopying clause, 'Reproduced with permission from *Parachute Fun for Everyone* published by BRF 2011 (978 1 84101 702 0)', so long as reproduction is for use in a teaching situation by the original purchaser. The right to photocopy material is not granted for anyone other than the original purchaser without written permission from BRF.

The Copyright Licensing Agency (CLA)

If you are resident in the UK and you have a photocopying licence with the Copyright Licensing Agency (CLA), please check the terms of your licence. If your photocopying request falls within the terms of your licence, you may proceed without seeking further permission. If your request exceeds the terms of your CLA licence, please contact the CLA direct with your request. Copyright Licensing Agency, 90 Tottenham Court Road, London W1T 4LP. Telephone 020 7631 5555; fax 020 7631 5500; email cla@cla.co.uk; website www.cla.co.uk. The CLA will provide photocopying authorisation and royalty fee information on behalf of BRF.

BRF is a Registered Charity (No. 233280)

Contents

Gospel stories

✻

Foreword

The use of parachutes for play is certainly not a new tool for children's leaders. The very first play parachutes were real ones, with heavy webbing and stitching that would cope with the most rigorous play sessions. As the idea caught on, so did the manufacture of chutes especially for play. These new lightweight, multicoloured chutes grew in popularity and inspired teachers, youth leaders and children's workers to incorporate parachute play into their regular play sessions. The variety of play parachutes, together with the flexibility of use for hundreds of games, challenges and activities, means that parachute play is here to stay.

I remember the very first time I played with a parachute and saw the wonder and excitement on the faces of the children. From that very first experience I rated parachutes very high on the squeal factor—that is, the amount of audible squeal you hear as the children play.

Parachute Fun for Everyone is a 'must have' book for all who work with children, because Renita has managed to incorporate all the excitement of parachute play with a wide collection of relevant Bible stories that will not only help children engage more with the biblical narrative but will also rate high on the squeal factor.

My guess is that the number of games and applications within this book will inspire you to new levels of imagination in the use of parachutes in your regular children's meetings, clubs and groups. I am convinced that your children will not only derive a lot of pleasure from these games but, through playing them, will grow deeper in their knowledge and love of God. ENJOY!

Duncan Dyason
Chair of Trustees, Street Kids Direct, author and children's work leader

✳

Introduction

Playchutes (parachutes designed for play) are multi-coloured, multi-age, multi-fun. They enhance education, encourage teamwork, improve fitness, facilitate communication and provide hours of enthusiastic entertainment. They are also naturally shaped for group gatherings and promote core values: everyone participates, everyone belongs and everyone takes care of each other.

Parachute Fun for Everyone is for anyone who wants to use a chute in telling, teaching and worship. It is packed with pick-and-mix activities: stories, songs, prayers, reflections and games. Each activity is simply explained and can stand alone or be connected to others for easy programme planning. The book is indexed by title and activity type. Photographs of some of the games can be found on the Barnabas website, www.barnabasinchurches.org.uk/pdfs/parachutefun.pdf, or at http://renitaboyle.com.

The playchute practicalities below will help you choose a chute, use it safely, plan a programme and adapt activities for all ages and abilities. Useful resources are also noted.

A playchute can be a river, a rippling lake, a hurricane or a storm stilled; the Red Sea to divide, a mountain to climb or a desert to wander through; a shipwreck or an island. It can be Noah's ark, Jonah's whale, the temple, the stable or the tomb; Joseph's coat, the Samaritan woman's well or Jesus' grave clothes. It can be a deep-sea dive, fishing net, field for scattered seeds or the breeze that scatters them. A playchute can tell the story of creation, Advent, Easter, Pentecost and the gospel. It can be raised to the glory of God or lowered in humble prayer.

Whether you are working with pre-schoolers, primaries, tweens, teenagers or adults; in nurseries or nursing homes, camps, clubs or churches, Sunday schools, schools or with special needs; at assemblies, community festivals, family days, spiritual retreats or training days, parachute fun is for everyone!

Playchute practicalities

Choosing a playchute and accessories

Playchutes come in a variety of sizes:

- small six-handle pre-school chutes: 180cm or less (6 ft)
- medium: 350–600cm (12–20 ft), ideal for an average class
- large: 900cm (30 ft)
- massive 42-handle chutes for large groups: 1200cm or above (40 ft)

They are usually round, with multi-coloured segments or target-like in design. Speciality chutes include those with plastic portholes or picture pockets, mathematic or language educhutes, smiling faces, pumpkins or the rectangular rainbow ripple complete with bouncing stars. White parachutes can be decorated with fabric pens and paint (see page 20) and some chutes have a large hole in the middle for wheelchair users.

You might also want to consider an Octaband™. This looks like a colourful stretchy octopus and can be used in any sized space. It works well for all ages and abilities but is particularly ideal for group work among wheelchair users and others whose upper-body abilities may differ from one another. It allows for individual movement while maintaining the communal feel of a traditional chute.

One playchute is great; two are even better for combined activities or managing large groups. Playchutes can be purchased through educational websites and catalogues or can be custom-made for quality, size and personalised design.

A useful guide in terms of size is 1.5 players per section of chute. However, the chute you choose will ultimately depend on the age, size and needs of your group and the size of your playing area. It is worth noting that large chutes can be rolled up smaller, but small chutes can't be made bigger.

Other useful accessories include foam balls, bell balls, streamer balls, beach balls and earth balls; bean bags, foam dice and disks; scarves, Frisbees, ribbons, hoops, ropes and stuffed toys. Simple instruments are also useful: ankle bells, shakers, drums, triangles, cymbals, xylophones, slide whistles, thunder makers and basic stringed instruments. You can also use bed sheets or nylon fabric if needs must.

See the resources section on page 127 for details on how to obtain all of the above.

Using your playchute safely

The first rule of thumb when it comes to safety is to know your group and their individual needs. Identify a leader who will bear ultimate responsibility for safe play and a smooth running programme. Both are more easily achieved with preparation and help, particularly if you are playing with young children or in groups of mixed abilities. Carers should take responsibility for their own children, and spotters should be assigned to gather objects and otherwise assist. Encourage peers to help vulnerable participants where possible and offer support to the degree that is needed. Ensure a good helper-to-child ratio and check that everyone is happy with bending, sitting, stretching and floor work. Adapt activities if necessary (see below).

Give clear instructions and set boundaries. Everyone should be aware and take care: all are mutually responsible for safe play. No one should run on top of the chute or be trapped underneath. Shoes should be removed when crawling on the chute, unless otherwise stated. Only a few players should be allowed under the chute at any one time. Vulnerable participants should be accompanied on to or under the chute to avoid panic.

The easiest grip for most activities is both hands in front, thumbs down. Limbs should be kept out of handles, and heads out of the centre hole (if there is one). Agree a signal for 'stop', which anyone can use, and avoid higher-risk activities unless there is established trust within the group. Emphasise cooperation rather than competition. Remind everyone regularly about safety.

Plan your programme (see below) in advance. Some activities can be safely done in a classroom, but most require enough space for the chute to lie flat and players to run safely around it. Soft surfaces are best; grass should be dry and floors splinter-free.

Gather evenly around the chute in terms of spacing and ability. It works well to start and stop with the chute grounded. Gauge the height of the chute to suit the smallest player. Be as inclusive as possible. Allow people to opt out until they are comfortable opting in. Practising new moves before play helps to build confidence and prevent accidents.

Keep the chute in a pillowcase for easier access. To avoid a scramble, lay it open before everyone arrives or choose a small group of helpers. To put it away, loft the chute, let go and whisk it away in theme (for example, 'the Holy Spirit moves where he will') or involve everyone in rolling it up (for example, 'let's make a tiny mustard seed').

Playchute fabric is highly flammable and can pose a suffocation hazard. Ensure that any objects being used do not pose a choking hazard for the group you are working with.

Much of the advice given under 'Adapting playchute activities for all ages and abilities' will also be useful for general use.

To play safely and well:

- Know your group.
- Identify your team.
- Plan your programme.
- Adapt activities.
- Choose a suitable space.
- Avoid a scramble.
- Gather evenly.
- Include everyone.
- Encourage peer support.

- Begin and end with the chute grounded.
- Give clear instructions.
- Agree a signal for 'stop' and 'quiet'.
- Be aware and take care.
- No one should run on top.
- No one should be trapped underneath.
- Take shoes off to crawl on top.
- Allow only a few underneath at a time.
- Make sure vulnerable participants are accompanied.
- Gauge the height of the chute to suit the smallest player.
- Use handles properly.
- Warm up and cool down.
- Put out and away in theme.
- Keep the chute away from fire.
- Ensure that props are user-safe.

Planning your programme

The activities in *Parachute Fun for Everyone* can stand alone or be connected with each other. You may also want to use them in a wider context than this resource allows. Whether you are looking for a simple song for under-fives, a five-minute story for school assembly, an hour's activity in a busy club or a quiet retreat with adults, it is helpful to reflect on the following questions when planning your programme:

- Who are our leaders?
  * Do we all know each other? Does everyone work well together? Do we all know what we are doing?

- Who is in our group?
  * Are they well-known or new? What is their age range and ability? Does the group have a specific purpose? Is it sacred or secular?

- What size is our group?
  - ✲ Do we need to divide into two groups and use two chutes rather than one? Which activities are best for the numbers involved?
- What is our theme?
  - ✲ What is the story we need for today? What is our focus? How will we explore it?
- What do we need?
  - ✲ Do we need activities that are reflective or energetic, for inside or outside, a single activity for an established programme or a whole programme? What kind of resources and accessories are required?
- Where will we be?
  - ✲ Are the playing space and setting suitable? What are the safety issues and weather alternatives?
- How can we be inclusive?
  - ✲ Can we involve everyone, adapt activities to suit abilities, respect the feelings of those who may be reluctant, and welcome group ideas?
- How do we make up teams?
  - ✲ Can we divide by theme: sun, moon, stars; those with blue eyes or brown; birthday months? Can the players divide themselves?
- How can we be sensitive?
  - ✲ How can we keep our focus on the person, not the programme; give the group space to explore and respond?
- How will we minimise disruptive behaviour?
  - ✲ Shall we give time out or change the activity? How will we clearly communicate the boundaries?

Adapting playchute activities for all ages and abilities

The activities in *Parachute Fun for Everyone* are suitable for general use, from children in primary and elementary schools through to adults. Many activities are already suitable for mixed abilities and most can be adapted.

Much of the guidance given below is also applicable for those working with under-fives whose confidence and competence will grow with time. In general, smaller chutes, simplified actions and short, quieter activities involving repetition and rhyme will work best with under-fives. See resources on page 127 for some good general books on using playchutes with early years.

The general benefits of using a playchute are increased for those with mobility issues or developmental needs. Playchute activities enhance physical fitness, flexibility, agility, strength and coordination. They promote turn-taking, team spirit and problem-solving and create a sense of achievement, cooperation and community.

Playchute activities are visually stimulating, experiential and tactile: rustling, rippling, wafting and waving, breezing. They appeal across ages, ability levels and learning styles, break down literacy barriers and create a comfortable environment for inclusive play and learning.

Some participants (or entire groups) may need close individual supervision. As there will be varying degrees of independence, support should be offered to the degree that it is needed. Encourage peers to help where possible: wheelchairs can be pushed during activities that require quick movement. Those unable to participate easily often enjoy lying or sitting on top of or under the chute while the activity is performed by others. This requires a high level of trust. Ensure that vulnerable participants feel safe and comfortable and are accompanied to avoid sudden panic.

Be aware of how participants are responding to the chute

itself. Some will find it immediately attractive; others will find it threatening. Prior exposure and clear communication about what to expect can minimise uncertainty and enhance the experience for all concerned.

Those with visual impairment may be easily startled by the sounds of the chute and will have little concept of it beyond what they can touch. A tour around the chute, under and on top, will give some idea of its size. Continue to communicate what is happening as the activity progresses. Those with hearing impairment will also appreciate clear communication and added time to grasp instructions.

Participants with behavioural or attention difficulties may be overwhelmed or overstimulated by the chute. Prior preparation and communication will be beneficial. Boundaries should be clearly and simply stated. Allow time for adjustment to the environment and participation on a level that is comfortable. Focus on making the experience positive and enjoyable. Manage behaviour, where possible, through a change of activity, and make good use of activities that are reflective.

Wheelchair users of all ages will appreciate a height adjustment in activities. This will naturally occur in groups where everyone is in a wheelchair, such as nursing homes or residential care. Where there is a single wheelchair user, gauge the height of the chute to suit—or, for a truly inclusive experience, consider asking everyone to sit in a chair. Many activities will work equally well from a sitting position.

You may also want to adjust the activity itself. Instead of running around with the chute, you could stay where you are and pass the chute from hand to hand. If actions are too complicated or too many, simplify them and limit their number. Offer help with parts of an activity that can't be achieved alone, incorporate physical suggestions that can, or offer an alternative. Ensure that any objects being used do not pose a choking hazard for the group you are working with.

You may want to consider a wheelchair-specific chute or an Octaband™ (see 'Choosing a playchute and accessories' on page 11). Octabands™ work particularly well with groups whose upper-body abilities differ, and they can be used in any sized space. They are ideal for worship activities that involve music and movement.

Be flexible where structured activities are not easily achieved. Focus on the person, not the programme. Aim for every participant to have a positive experience and to feel good about their participation.

Turn the chute itself into an art project. Attach ribbons, streamers and bells to the handles. Personalise it with fabric pens and paints. Attach plastic pockets and display artwork, story scenes or memory verses.

Enhance activities with props, crafts and music. Bounce balloons, blow bubbles, include simple instruments when telling stories, and play background music. Use crafts, water balloons, flashlights and torches.

You can also use your chute as a tent, a target, a curtain, a screen, a giant ball pool or a blanket.

- Be particularly aware of safety.
- Ensure close supervision by trusted adults.
- Support should be offered to the degree that it is needed.
- Encourage peers to help where possible.
- Allow time to adjust to the environment.
- Allow participation as and when it feels comfortable.
- Accompany vulnerable participants on to or under the chute.
- Ensure that participants feel safe.
- Offer prior exposure to the chute where possible.
- Clearly communicate what to expect before play.
- Continue to communicate what is happening as the activity progresses.
- Manage behaviour with a change of activity.
- Gauge the height of the chute to suit, or all sit in chairs.

- Simplify action songs and activities.
- Offer help for actions that can't be achieved alone.
- Move the chute rather than the person.
- Consider a wheelchair-friendly chute or an Octaband™.
- Be flexible where structure is not easily achieved.
- Focus on the person, a positive experience and the feel-good factor.
- Turn your chute into an art project.
- Enhance the activities with props, crafts and music.
- Use your chute as a tent, a target, a curtain, a screen or a giant ball pool.

✱

Decorate a chute

If you do not already have a playchute or are thinking of adding another, why not decorate your own? All you need is a white playchute, fabric markers and paint and a little group imagination. Paint the days of creation, Noah's animals, an underwater scene, episodes from the life of Jesus, handprints, footprints or thumbprints, or scenes from Christmas or Easter.

You can also easily enhance the chute you have. Attach ribbons, streamers and bells to the handles. Personalise it with fabric pens and paints. Attach plastic pockets and display artwork, story scenes or memory verses.

Stories from Genesis

God's creation

Bible background

Genesis 1:1—2:25

Theme

God creates the world in six days and rests on the seventh.

Activity summary

This is a step-inside story. It could stand alone as a 45-minute session. It involves activities that are both energetic and reflective.

For part of this story, the chute will be used in a three-dimensional collage. The collage will cover the surface area of your chute; it will be created gradually and will involve everyone as the story unfolds. Some people will also play simple musical instruments on cue.

You could gather or make collage materials together before the session. Keep the story itself a surprise until it is time to tell it.

You will need:
- Story script
- Collage materials (divided into easily accessible containers):
  * Sky (light blue)
  * Light (yellow or orange)
  * Sea (dark blue, turquoise or sea green)
  * Land (brown, tan or green)
  * Plants (trees, vegetables, flowers and fruit—make sure you include a tree of knowledge and a tree of life)
  * Stars (confetti and group-made stars)
  * Sea creatures and birds (group-made paper fish and birds)

- Props:
  - ✴ Streamer balls (bright plastic balls with ribbon tails)
  - ✴ Sun (hula hoop with golden tinsel)
  - ✴ Moon (hula hoop with silver tinsel)

- Instruments:
  - ✴ Deep-sounding drums (darkness and deep water)
  - ✴ Wind chimes ('and God whispered')
  - ✴ Cymbals (starburst)

- Reflective instrumental music

Parachute fun!

This story will work best if you are familiar with it. Begin with everyone seated around the chute. Choose instrumentalists. The teller stands on the chute.

Teller: Once before a time, there was a beginning… and before the beginning was God. Everywhere was darkness (*all cover eyes with hands*) and deep water (*beat drums or thighs slowly*).

God's Spirit moved over the water (*hold chute: ripple gently; the leader stays in the middle*).

Then God said, 'Let there be light!' (*wind chimes*). And there was light!

Light burst: the leader joins the circle. Stand and hold the chute mid-height, sagging, thumbs up. Toss the streamer balls on to the chute. On the count of one, ripple gently; two, moderately; three, energetically. Try to keep the balls on the chute. Choose a helper to collect those that fall off and return them. Stop play and create a final single burst by

Reproduced with permission from *Parachute Fun for Everyone* published by BRF 2011 (978 1 84101 702 0)
www.barnabasinchurches.org.uk

launching the balls into the air on the count of three. Shout 'Let there be light!' and play the cymbals. Sit around the chute again.

Teller: 'This is good!' God said. *(All repeat)*

God made light and dark: morning *(wind chimes)* and night *(beat drums/thighs slowly)*. This was the first day.

On the second day, God made a dome and called it 'sky'.

Sky dome: stand and hold the chute mid-height, thumbs down. Loft the chute and look up into the dome. After the final time, ground the chute and sit around it.

Teller: There was deep space above the sky and deep water below it.

Single rolling wave: all stand and hold the chute mid-height, thumbs down. One person after another lifts and lowers the chute to create a wave. Ground the chute and sit around its edge.

Teller: 'This is good!' God said. *(All repeat)*

On the third day, God gathered all the water together and dry ground appeared: 'land' and 'sea'.

Use the sky, sea and land materials to create a chute collage. Sit around the edge and admire your creation.

Teller: 'This is good!' God said. *(All repeat)*

Then God made everything that grows—plants, trees, flowers, fruit, vegetables, vines and grain—each with seeds so that there would always be new growth.

Add plant materials to your collage. Include a tree of life and a tree of knowledge, though you will not be mentioning them in this story. Sit down and admire your creation.

Teller: 'This is good!' God said. *(All repeat)*

On day four, God made the sun and the moon.

Choose two people opposite each other to be the sun and moon. Send them skipping around in opposite directions with hoops held high. When they return to their places, add the sun and moon hoops to the collage.

Teller: God also made the stars *(add crafted stars and confetti)*. 'This is good!' God said. *(All repeat)*

On the fifth day, God made everything that flies and swims. He blessed them all and told them to live everywhere.

Add sea creatures and birds to your collage using the sea creatures. Sit around the edge and admire your creation.

Teller: 'This is good!' God said. *(All repeat)*

On the sixth day, God made all the land animals: tame and wild, creeping and climbing.

Add animals to your collage. Sit around the edge and admire your creation.

Teller: 'This is good!' God said. *(All repeat)*

Then God made the first people *(choose an Adam and Eve to come on to the chute and crouch down)*. God made a man *(touch Adam's head; he grows into a man)*. God made a woman *(touch Adam's rib; Eve grows into a woman)*.

God blessed the first people. 'You will be like me,' God said. 'It is your job to take care of everything. You will have plenty to eat and be blessed in everything.'

The man and woman sit down where they are on the chute.

Teller: Then God looked at everything he made. 'This is VERY good!' God said. *(All repeat)*

And on the seventh day... God rested.

Reflections

What did it feel like to create this universe together? How do you think it felt to be the first people? Why were they special? In what ways do we care for the planet? Why are rest days important? How do we rest?

Involve everyone in carefully taking the creation apart and returning the props to their boxes.

Connections

This theme connects with:
- Adam's apple (see page 27)
- The wonders of God (see page 59)
- Sea stills (see page 66)
- Wonderfully made (see page 70)
- Come, praise the Lord (see page 72)
- Thanks for everything (see page 86)

Adam's apple

Bible background

Genesis 2:9—3:24

Theme

Sin separates.

Activity summary

This is a reflective seek-and-find story starter and collage.

You will need:
- Collage materials as for 'God's creation' (see page 22)
- Things to hide within the collage, such as butterflies, stuffed animals, flowers, rubbery bugs, and so on
- A list of what you've hidden (for yourself)
- Fresh fruit for each person
- Paper apples with sweets attached (these could be previously made by the group)
- Your own version of the Bible story

Parachute fun!

Lay out a creation collage on the chute before the session. Be sure to include a tree of life, a tree of knowledge and a serpent. Put the fresh fruit on to the tree of life and the apple sweets on the tree of knowledge. Hide the other items in the collage.

Gather the group around the chute. Tell them what to seek and find. Emphasise that they can go anywhere on the chute, but must not touch the tree of knowledge. Gather together again and tell your own version of the story.

Reflections

Use the fruit and sweets to emphasise the two special trees in the garden. One was good and led to life (being close to God and living God's way). The other was bad and led to death (looked good but led to distance from God and living our own way). Although we make choices that aren't good for us, God still wants us to have abundant life (John 10:10). We can choose to live God's way. Share the fruit and sweets together.

Connections

This theme connects with:
- God's creation (see page 22)
- Scrubbed clean (see page 64)
- One way (see page 92)
- I am (see page 93)
- A full life (see page 112)

Noah's boat

Bible background

Genesis 6:5—9:17

Theme

Noah believes God and builds a big boat.

Activity summary

This is an energetic story starter which involves a chant, crossover game and instruments.

You will need:
- Percussion instruments (optional)
- Your own version of the Bible story

You will also need to learn the following two-part chant:

A: Noah built a boat, built a big, big boat *(loft the chute, thumbs down; take one step under)*; Noah built a big, big boat *(lower the chute behind your bum; lean forward)*.
B: I wonder will it float, will it float, float, float *(hold chute mid-height in front of you, thumbs down)*; I wonder will it float, float, float? *(shake chute vigorously)*

Parachute fun!

Sit around the chute. Practise the words and rhythm of the chant. Choose instrumentalists (optional). Stand and hold the chute mid-height, in front of you, thumbs under. Add the actions to the chant (for variety, change the volume and action, for example, whisper and make ripples).

Now add a game of animal crossovers. Identify two people to be each kind of animal: kangaroos (jump), rabbits (hop), elephants (make a trunk with arm), giraffe (make a neck with arm overhead), fish (hands together, swimming), bugs (bulging eyes), birds (flying), pigs (push nose up), lions (roar) and so on. The leader calls out one or two pairs, who swap places under the chute while everyone else holds it high. The chant is repeated between each round of crossovers until everyone is exhausted. Collapse on to the chute and tell your own version of the Bible story.

Reflections

Can you think of a time when you or someone you know believed what God had said but nobody else did?

Connections

This theme connects with:

- Rise up and stand firm (see page 60)
- Sing of God's love (see page 69)

Father Abraham

Bible background

Genesis 15 and 17—18; 21:1–8

Theme

God promises Abraham a son and more descendants than the number of the stars.

Activity summary

This is an energetic story starter based on the popular action song 'Father Abraham had many sons' (author and copyright unknown). Find the lyrics and tune at www.kididdles.com/lyrics/f033.html.

You will need:

- A few percussion instruments (optional)
- Your own version of the Bible story

Parachute fun!

Distribute instruments to those not otherwise participating. Stand, hold the chute mid-height in front of you, arms crossed, thumbs down. Waft it up and down to the rhythm of the music during the chorus. Add one action after the other until you are doing everything.

Song chorus *(waft chute up and down)*:

Father Abraham had many sons,
Many sons had Father Abraham.
I am one of them and so are you,
So let's all praise the Lord.

Right arm *(release right hand, raise right arm, turn out and return)*.
Left arm *(release left hand, raise left arm, turn out and return)*.
Right leg *(shake right leg and return)*.
Left leg *(shake left leg and return)*.
Nod your head *(nod)*.
Turn around *(turn 360 degrees, changing hands)*.
Sit down *(sit down, ground chute)*.

Reflections

Tell the story as you think best for your group. What can we do to believe God's promises even when they seem unimaginable?

Connections

Use this activity as part of a 'starry telling' night. Find the constellations. Talk about creation. If you can't be outside, look at a map of the star system and make shiny stars. Write the names of some of Abraham's descendants on the stars and include yourself. Sing 'Twinkle, twinkle, little star' with the chute and launch stars into the air.

This theme also connects with:
* Rise up and stand firm (see page 60)
* Sing of God's love (see page 69)

Esau's silly sip

Bible background

Genesis 25:27–34

Theme

Esau sells his birthright for a sip of bean stew.

Activity summary

This is a moderate-energy story that involves a chant, props, role play and story cards.

You will need:
- A large cauldron and spoon
- A basket containing eight vegetables with numbered story cards attached to them
- The chant and story script

Parachute fun!

Ground the chute and gather around it. The teller stands in the middle with the vegetable basket, pot and spoon. Choose a Jacob and eight clear readers. Each reader takes a vegetable from the basket (in numerical order), reads the card and puts the vegetable in the pot.

Jacob stirs the pot while everyone else ripples the chute and chants: 'Bubble and boil, stirring the pot, Jacob wants what Esau's got!'

Reader 1: All brothers argue, but Jacob and Esau fought even before they were born. *(Chant)*

Reader 2: God said that each would lead a great nation but one would be stronger—and the older twin would serve the younger. *(Chant)*

Reader 3: Esau was a strong and hairy hunter. Jacob was a quiet cook. *(Chant)*

Reader 4: One day, Esau came back from hunting with empty hands and a rumbling tummy. He smelled Jacob's yummy stew and said, 'Give me some stew! I'm starving!' *(Chant)*

Reader 5: Now, Esau had something that Jacob wanted—a special right that was his because he was the oldest. *(Chant)*

Reader 6: Esau would be the head of the family when their father died, and twice as wealthy as Jacob. *(Chant)*

Reader 7: 'Let's trade,' said Jacob. 'You can have some of my stew now, if you give me your birthright later.' *(Chant)*

Reader 8: So Esau traded his birthright for a sip of bean stew and some bread, and Jacob knew that he would be a very rich man. *(Chant)*

Reflections

You might want to think about how Jacob gave up his future blessing to satisfy an immediate hunger. How was this wise or unwise? How do we do this in our own lives?

Connections

You could use this activity to promote Fairtrade awareness or host a soup lunch.

Reproduced with permission from *Parachute Fun for Everyone* published by BRF 2011 (978 1 84101 702 0)
www.barnabasinchurches.org.uk

* ✱ *

Jacob's ladder

Bible background

Genesis 28:1–22; 1 Corinthians 3:16

Theme

Jacob has visitors and a vision.

Activity summary

This is an energetic story starter followed by a reflective story. It involves call-and-response, instruments and props and includes a craft.

You will need:
- A slide whistle or xylophone
- One stone for the leader (which will act as a pillow)
- One stone per child (optional)
- A tiny bottle of oil
- Paints or marker pens
- Worship music

Parachute fun!

Distribute the slide whistle or xylophone to someone who might not otherwise participate. Count off by twos around the chute: 'angels going up' and 'angels going down'. The leader is 'Gabriel'.

Hold the chute high and taut. When Gabriel calls 'angels going up', those going up weave clockwise in and out of the others around the chute and back to their spaces (while the slide whistle or xylophone plays up the scale).

34

When Gabriel calls 'angels going down', those going down weave anti-clockwise as above (while the slide whistle or xylophone plays down the scale).

When Gabriel calls 'God is at the top', everyone lofts the chute together and looks into the dome.

When you have finished, ground the chute and gather around it. The leader uses the stone and oil to tell the story.

Story

Jacob had been travelling and was tired. He laid his head on a large stone and went to sleep (all nestle under the chute; leader lays head on stone). Jacob dreamed about a ladder resting on the earth, with its top reaching into heaven. Angels were going up and down and God was standing at the top.

God promised that Jacob and his people would be blessed— that God would look after him wherever he went. When Jacob woke up, he said, 'Surely the Lord is in this place' (all wake up and sit up).

Jacob poured oil on the stone he had used for a pillow and named the place Bethel (leader does this reverently). Bethel means 'the house of the Lord'.

Reflections

Have you ever had a comforting dream? How do you think this dream helped Jacob through difficult times? How do you know when a place is a special 'house of the Lord'?

Discuss the idea that a special place of God is wherever God speaks to us. Talk about what this means: 'You are a temple of the living God' (1 Corinthians 3:16). Think about a special place or time when God spoke to you. Paint the stones and write the verse on them. Use the stones as a reminder.

Connections

This story is also a picture of what Jesus has done for us, by coming to earth to make a way into heaven. See also 'Jacob's tussle' below.

Jacob's tussle

Bible background

Genesis 32:22–32

Theme

Jacob grabs hold of God, gets a new name and goes a bit lame.

Activity summary

This is an energetic story starter that involves a pillow fight, tug of war and standing still on signal.

You will need:
- A bell, a triangle and a whistle
- Three pillows
- Your own version of the story

Parachute fun!

Ground the chute and use it as an arena for a pillow fight. Choose two players. Give each player a pillow for their right hand and one to hold between them in their left. They must try to get their opponent to let go of the pillow in their left hand while hitting them with the pillow in the right.

For a whole-group game, roll the chute up lengthwise and use it like a rope in a game of tug of war.

Give the bell and triangle to people who might find it difficult to participate otherwise. Ring the bell to freeze everyone in their position. Resume play with a ting of the triangle. The leader blows the whistle to stop play, get attention or choose new players.

Reflections

Tell your own version of the story. Jacob wrestled the whole night with God, and God blessed him for his determination. How can we take hold of God and never let him go?

Connections

This theme connects with:
• Jacob's ladder (see page 34)

Joseph's coat

Bible background

Genesis 37; 39—45 and 50
Joseph gets into big bother with his brothers; God brings the best out of the worst.

Activity summary

This is an energetic story that involves call-and-response and a game of crossovers.

You will need:
• Story script

Parachute fun!

Hold the chute mid-height, thumbs down. Count off around the chute with the following colours: green, red, black, blue and silver. Tell the story. Everyone shakes the chute on the word 'Coat', sits down on 'White' and swaps places under the lofted chute when their own colour is called.

Story

Joseph was Jacob's favourite son, so Jacob made Joseph a colourful COAT. Joseph's eleven older brothers were GREEN with envy.

Joseph told his brothers about a dream he had. They were all bundles of grain. 'Mine stood up,' Joseph said, 'and yours bowed down to mine.' The brothers were RED with anger.

Joseph had another dream. The sun, moon and eleven SILVER stars bowed down to him. The brothers went RED with anger.

One day, the brothers saw Joseph coming in his COAT. They were GREEN with envy and RED with anger. They took Joseph's COAT and threw him into a BLACK pit. Joseph felt BLUE.

Joseph's brothers then took him out of the BLACK pit and sold him to slave traders for 20 SILVER coins. They put goat's blood on his COAT. Jacob thought Joseph was dead and felt BLUE.

Joseph was alive in Egypt. Pharaoh had a BLACK dream. Joseph told him a great hunger was coming, and Joseph was put in charge of storing grain.

When the hunger came, Jacob sent his sons to buy grain. They didn't know Joseph but Joseph knew them. Joseph found out that his brothers felt BLUE about what they had done. They were no longer RED with anger or GREEN with envy.

Joseph had missed his brothers and still loved them, so he gave them grain for free. He told them he forgave them and they felt all WHITE inside.

(Quick fire round)
Joseph had a cool COAT. His brothers were GREEN, saw RED and threw him into a BLACK pit. Joseph was BLUE, sold for SILVER but stored grain. His brothers were forgiven and everything was all WHITE!

Reflections

Think about Joseph's words: 'You tried to harm me, but God made it turn out for the best, so that he could save all these people, as he is now doing' (Genesis 50:20). In what situations has God ever brought something good out of bad for us today?

Connections

Joseph helped people in need. Participate in a community project for a local charity or a global campaign to make life better for those in poverty.

This theme also connects with:
- Benjamin's cup (see page 40)
- Scrubbed clean (see page 64)
- A full life (see page 112)

Benjamin's cup

Bible background

Genesis 44—45

Theme

Benjamin is set up as he sets out for home.

Activity summary

This is a moderate-energy story starter and story combined. It involves props, story cards and music, and includes a craft.

You will need:
- Eleven pillowcases (grain bags)
- Shredded paper (grain) to half-fill each pillowcase
- A silver cup
- Other items could include rat, snake, mouse, chocolate coins, sunglasses, gummy creatures, teddies, spider, frog, bat and so on
- Numbered story cards as below
- Music

Before the session, half-fill eleven pillowcases (grain bags) with shredded paper (grain). Place the cup and story cards in one bag. Divide the other items between the remaining bags. Tie each bag shut with an elastic band.

Parachute fun!

Kneel around the chute. Hold it low in both hands, thumbs down. Heap the bags on to the chute, start the music and shake the chute.

Stop the music and choose a 'servant' to guess which bag the cup is in. Remove the bag from play if it is found not to contain the cup. Continue play, changing the servant each time, until you have found the cup and story cards. Distribute the story cards to confident readers. Tell the story.

Story cards

1. During a time of great hunger, Benjamin and his brothers went to Egypt to buy food. Their brother Joseph was in charge, but they didn't recognise him. The older brothers had sold him into slavery and pretended he was dead. They never expected to see him again.

2. Benjamin was the youngest. Joseph loved Benjamin and wanted him to stay in Egypt. He wanted to protect Benjamin from his cruel brothers, so Joseph played a trick to see if they had changed.

3. After filling their bags with grain, Joseph told a servant to hide his special silver cup in Benjamin's bag. He wanted it to look as though Benjamin had stolen it.

4. In the morning, the brothers loaded their donkeys and headed home. Joseph told the servant to go after them and accuse them of stealing his special silver cup.

5. The brothers were shocked and confused. They knew they were innocent but promised that if the cup was found in one of their bags, whoever owned that bag would die and the others would become slaves.

6. Each brother opened his bag while the servant searched. The last bag belonged to Benjamin—and in it was Joseph's cup. Just imagine how everyone felt!

7. When they got back to the palace, the brothers threw themselves down before Joseph. 'What can we say?' said Judah. 'How can we prove that we are innocent? Now you will kill our brother and the rest of us will be your slaves.'

8. It had been Judah's idea to sell Joseph as a slave. Although he seemed like a changed person, Joseph wanted to make sure. 'I wouldn't do that,' he said. 'Only the one who had the cup will become my slave. The rest of you can go home to your father.'

9. Judah was brave and wanted to save Benjamin. He volunteered to take his place. 'How can I go back to my father without him?' he said. 'I couldn't bear my father's misery!' Joseph knew then that his brothers had become loving and kind.

10. Joseph just couldn't keep his secret any longer. He told his brothers who he really was and wept so loudly that everyone in the palace could hear him. His brothers were shocked.

11. Joseph forgave them. Even though his brothers had hurt him, God had had other plans for good. Joseph was able to offer them food and a new and better life. He hugged all of his brothers. He told them to go home and come back with their father.

Reflections

How do we show our families that we love them? What are some good ways of showing that we forgive each other? What occasions can we think of when we were relieved to tell the truth?

Connections

Joseph's cup was special because it was a symbol of his power in Egypt. Paint a cup with symbols of things that are important to you.

This theme also connects with:
• Joseph's coat (see page 37)

Moses
activities

Moses in the basket

Bible background

Exodus 2:1–10; 6:20

Theme

Baby boy found bobbing in a basket.

Activity summary

This story starter is a reflective rocking activity. It can be very therapeutic but should only be done if there is appropriate supervision and established trust within the group.

You will need:
- Teddies (optional)
- Your own version of the story

Parachute fun!

Fold the chute into a layered rectangle. This should make a hammock (basket). Choose a baby Moses (teddy/person) to lie on the folded chute. Several participants lift the chute and rock Moses gently.

When you have finished, ground the chute and invite everyone to lie under it as if it were a blanket. Tell the story as you think best for your group.

Reflections

You might want to reflect on the compassion of the princess or how God had an amazing plan for Moses even when he was a baby.

Connections

This theme connects with:
- Other Moses activities (see pages 45–56)

Moses in a rage

Bible background

Exodus 1:11–15

Theme

Moses acts in anger and ends up in a hot desert.

Activity summary

This is a moderate-energy story starter involving role play, music and a craft.

You will need:
- Bricks made from shoeboxes (at least one per person; the more the better)
- One red shoebox brick
- Dramatic instrumental music
- Your own version of the story

Parachute fun!

Ground the chute. The participants are slaves and build a tower on the chute with their bricks. Choose a master to boss them around and make things difficult. The slaves are not allowed to respond. Leave the last structure standing and gather everyone around the chute.

Play the music and pass the red brick around. When the music stops, the brick stops and the leader tells a bit of the story. Continue playing until the story is finished.

Reflections

Hold a discussion about the story, covering the following points.

- Moses was right to be angry but wrong to react.
- Moses experienced many feelings in this story (anger, compassion and fear).
- What are some things that make us feel angry, compassionate or afraid?
- How can we use our feelings to help others?

Connections

Decorate a brick to take home.

This theme connects with:
- Other Moses activities (see pages 44–56); see especially 'Moses, a bush and a snake' below

Moses, a bush and a snake

Bible background

Exodus 3:1–22; 4:1–17

Theme

God calls Moses to rescue his people.

Activity summary

This is a moderate-energy story starter followed by a reflective role play.

You will need:
- A skipping rope (snake)
- Flame-coloured scarves
- Your own version of the story

Parachute fun!

Hold the chute mid-height, thumbs down, and place a skipping rope (snake) on it. Shake the chute and try not to get bitten by the snake. When you have finished, ground the chute. Pick up the skipping rope and hold it taut to look like a stick.

Gather around the chute. Choose four participants to be the burning bush: stand back to back in the centre of the chute, waving scarves. Tell your own version of the story.

Choose a Moses to role-play the scene. Everyone should remove their shoes. Use the skipping rope as a staff, a snake and a staff again.

Reflections

Moses' stick was an everyday object, usually used to help him climb hills, but God used it in mighty ways. Moses thought that he couldn't do what God asked of him. God uses ordinary people to do extraordinary things. What do we feel God is calling us to do? What gives us courage?

Connections

This theme connects with:
- Other Moses activities (see pages 44–56). You can also use this activity with several skipping ropes to tell the Moses story in

Exodus 7:1–13. For additional Moses ideas, see *100 Children's Club Activities* by Jan Dyer (Kingsway, 2001), page 230.

Moses says, 'Let them go!'

Bible background

Exodus 7—12

Theme

Moses says, 'Let my people go!' Pharaoh says, 'No!'

Activity summary

This is an energetic story starter that culminates in a sober reflective time. It involves a chant and a series of games.

You will need:
- Torch or flashlight
- Ping-pong balls for hail (optional)
- Ribbon balls or flame-coloured scarves for fire (optional)

Parachute fun!

Chant

Leader: Moses said, 'Let them go!'
Players: Pharaoh said, 'No, no, no!'

Stand and hold the chute mid-height in both hands, thumbs down. Practise the chant and repeat it between each plague as below. The leader tells the story.

Story

The river turned to blood.

Passing wave: players holding one half of the chute lift and lower it to send a wave to the other half. The other half sends it back. Chant.

Frogs hopped.

Hold the chute low, and hop up and down. Chant.

Gnats nipped.

Hold the chute mid-height in your right hand. Gently tickle-nip the player on your left while trying not to be tickle-nipped by the player on your right. Chant.

Flies buzzed.

Hold the chute high in your left hand. Buzz around clockwise. Chant.

Animals died.

Ground the chute quickly and lie on top of it. Chant.

The Egyptians got itchy sores.

Hold the chute mid-height in your left hand, and scratch the back of the person on your right. Chant.

There was hail and fire.

Shake the chute mid-height in both hands, thumbs under. Use ping-pong balls for hail, and ribbon balls or scarves for fire. Chant.

Locusts ate the crops.

Munch the chute with your hands until you all meet in the middle. Chant.

The Egyptians were in the dark.

Close eyes. Chant.

But Pharaoh would still not listen, would not give up and would not let the people go.

Loft the chute and make a tent by sitting on its inside edge. A helper circles the outside of the tent, casting shadows with the torch or flashlight. Do this soberly.

At last, however, the oldest child in every Egyptian family, and the firstborn among their flocks, died. God's people, who had been constantly praying, were safe inside their houses where God told them to be—and were spared.

Reflections

Reflect on this story in a way that is best for your group.

Connections

This theme connects with:
* Other Moses activities (see pages 44–56)

Moses parts the sea

Bible background
Exodus 14:1–31

Theme
Pharaoh crosses God; God's people cross the sea.

Activity summary
This is a moderate-energy story starter.

You will need:
- Your own version of the story

Parachute fun!

Count the group off as 'Israelites' or 'Egyptians'. The 'Egyptians' stand, fold the chute in half and hold on to the long sides, forming a sagging U-shaped tunnel (Red Sea) between them. The 'Israelites' take turns crawling through the Red Sea while the Egyptians shake the chute and make sea sounds.

Change positions. The 'Egyptians' go through only once, as the sides of the chute lash down on them. Make sure no one feels unsafe or gets claustrophobic.

When you have finished, sit around the chute. Tell the story as you think best for your group.

Reflections
When Pharaoh let God's people go, they didn't even wait for their bread to rise. Can we think of any times when we had to hurry?

How might the Israelites have felt when they saw they were being followed... crossed the Red Sea... saw their enemies destroyed?

Connections

This theme connects with:

• Other Moses activities (see pages 44–56)

Miriam sings a song

Bible background

Exodus 15:19–21

Theme

Safely singing on the other side of the sea!

Activity summary

This is an energetic prayer of praise based on the traditional song 'I will sing unto the Lord' (author unknown). Complete lyrics and tune can be found at www.mypianoworld.com/MyPianoWorld-Praise/mypianoworldmoses.htm. The song can be sung in three parts, with three chutes turned into giant tambourines.

You will need:

• One chute (or three)
• Ankle bell (attachable with Velcro) for each person and chute handle
• Ribbons for each chute handle

Parachute fun!

Attach the streamers and bells to the participants and the chute(s). Stand around the chute(s) and hold it/them mid-height in your right hand.

Song

Move clockwise; jangle the chute to the beat as you sing.

I will sing unto the Lord for he has triumphed gloriously,
The horse and rider fell into the sea.

Repeat, changing hands and reversing direction.

The Lord my God, my strength, my song *(loft the chute)*,
Has now become my victory *(lower the chute)*.

Repeat.

The Lord is God and *(stomp)* I will praise him *(shake chute)*;
The Lord is God and I will exalt him *(loft and lower chute)*.

Repeat with two stomps on the last 'exalt'.

Reflections

Miriam sang these words when everyone had safely crossed the sea. Can we think of times when we were so happy that we felt like singing? How does singing help us? How does God feel when we praise him?

Connections

Create your own chute dances to familiar praise songs.

This theme connects with:
- Other Moses activities (see pages 44–56)
- Sing of God's love (see page 69)

Manna mayhem

Bible background

Exodus 16:13–36

Theme

God sends food from heaven.

Activity summary

This is an energetic story starter and gathering game.

You will need:

- Two chutes
- Manna and quail: cottonwool balls, packing peanuts or ping-pong balls (manna) and feathers (the more, the better)
- Your own version of the story

Parachute fun!

Divide into two groups and give each group a chute. Hold the chutes at mid-height. Put an equal measure of 'manna' and 'quail' on each chute; shake until they fall from heaven and scatter all over the desert (floor). Each team now holds their chute (basket) with one hand while gathering 'manna' and 'quail' into it with the other. The team who gathers the most wins. When you have finished, tell the story as you think best for your group.

Reflections

Have we ever been thankful for something and then got bored and started to complain about it? How can we remember to be thankful?

Connections

This theme connects with:

• Other Moses activities (see pages 44–56)

Ten targets

Bible background

Exodus 20:1–17; Matthew 22:37–39

Theme

Ten Commandments and one summary: 'Love God with all your heart, soul and mind… love others as much as you love yourself.'

Activity summary

This is an energetic reflection. The chute will act as a target for Frisbees, beanbags and balls.

You will need:

• Objects to toss (the more, the better): Frisbees, beanbags, balls

• Ten large unnumbered speech bubbles with one of the following commands written on each:
  ✻ Love God.
  ✻ Make God the most important person in your life.
  ✻ Always say God's name with love and respect.
  ✻ Set aside a day to celebrate God and to rest.
  ✻ Treat your parents with love and respect.
  ✻ Don't hurt anyone on purpose.
  ✻ Be faithful to your husband or wife.
  ✻ Don't take what doesn't belong to you.

* Tell the truth.
* Be happy with what you have.

- Two super-large speech bubbles with one of the most important commands written on each, as follows:
  * Love God with all your heart, soul and mind.
  * Love others as much as you love yourself.

Parachute fun!

Ground the chute and place the speech bubbles randomly on it. Keep the two 'most important commands' bubbles for later.

Explain the rules of the game. Everyone plays at the same time and must stand a good distance away from the chute. You must land a Frisbee, beanbag or ball on every speech bubble to win. Once you have landed an object, remove it so that others can keep trying. If you miss, you can keep trying. When time is up, gather around the outside edge of the chute and sit down.

Reflections

Did anyone hit all the targets? Do you think we can obey all of these commands all the time? There is chaos in the world because everyone misses the mark.

God gave the commands in an order: try to put the speech bubbles in order (see above for reference). Which is the most important? Jesus summarised the ten commands in just two. Bring out the two 'most important commands' bubbles and give the Bible reference (Matthew 22:37–39). Memorise the verse together and talk about how Jesus can help us to live God's way and how he can forgive us when we don't.

Connections

This theme connects with:
- The needle's eye (see page 104)

Psalms and a Proverb

God is my shield

Bible background

Psalm 18:1–7

Theme

David thanks God for protecting him.

Activity summary

This is an energetic reflection and ball game.

You will need:
- Two chutes
- Foam balls

Parachute fun!

Divide the group into two and put the teams on opposite sides of the playing area. One team will use their chute as a launcher and the other will use theirs as a shield. Place the balls on to the launcher and give a signal. The shield must try to catch as many balls as possible while shielding themselves under the chute, held high. Change groups and play again.

Reflections

David sang this song to the Lord on the day when he was rescued from his enemies and from Saul, who was trying to kill him. Talk about a time when you felt protected.

Memorise this verse: 'You are my mighty rock, my fortress, my protector, the rock where I am safe, my shield, my powerful weapon, and my place of shelter' (Psalm 18:2).

Connections

This theme connects with:
• Miriam sings a song (see page 52)

The wonders of God

Bible background

Psalm 19:1

Theme

The heavens keep telling the wonders of God, and the skies declare what he has done.

Activity summary

This is a reflective memory verse.

You will need:
• One chute

Parachute fun!

Hold the chute low with both hands in front of you. Chant Psalm 19:1 together as below.

The heavens keep telling *(loft the chute)*
the wonders of God *(lower the chute)*,
and the skies declare *(loft the chute)*
what he has done *(lower the chute)*.

Divide the group into two. One group lies under the chute while the other chants. Do it one last time together, loft the chute on the word 'done' and let go.

Reflections

How do you feel when you look at the stars? How do you think the heavens declare the wonders of God?

Connections

Write a creation psalm of your own and share it as part of a starry-telling night!

This theme connects with:
- God's creation (see page 22)
- Father Abraham (see page 30)

Rise up and stand firm

Bible background

Psalm 20:1–9

Theme

Trust in God, not in might.

Activity summary

This is a moderate-energy memory verse activity.

You will need:
- One chute

Parachute fun!

Attempt to stand up together, using the chute in the following way.

Players should be distributed evenly around the chute in terms of size and strength. Everyone sits down and holds the chute taut, with their arms out straight and knees tucked up between their bodies and the chute. Everyone's feet should be pressed flat together on the ground. On the count of three, chant the following verses and pull against each other to stand up. Reverse to sit down.

We trust in the name of the Lord our God...
we rise up and stand firm (*Psalm 20:7–8, NIV*).

Reflections

How do we help one another to 'rise up and stand firm' in our spiritual lives?

Connections

You could also use this activity to explore 1 Corinthians 12—what it means to work in unity as part of the body of Christ. Chant verse 27: 'Together you are the body of Christ. Each one of you is part of his body.'

Deep and wide

Bible background

Psalm 36:5–10

Theme

God's love is unfailing, his faithfulness unending.

Activity summary

This popular extension of an old action song can be energetic or reflective. Find the tune for 'Deep and wide' at www.hymnal.net/hymn.php/c/12 or in *Junior Praise* (35).

You will need:
• One chute

Parachute fun!

Hold the chute mid-height in front of you, thumbs down, as you sing the following action song.

Chorus (repeat twice between each verse)

Deep *(chute low and loose)* and wide *(chute high and taut)*
Deep *(chute low and loose)* and wide *(chute high and taut)*
There's a fountain flowing *(ripple chute)*
Deep *(chute low and loose)* and wide *(chute high and taut)*.

Verse 1 (repeat twice)

For me *(move in, meet in the middle)* and you *(move out)*
For me *(move in, meet in the middle)* and you *(move out)*
There's a fountain flowing *(ripple chute)*
Deep *(chute low and loose)* and wide *(chute high and taut)*.

Verse 2 (repeat twice)

Plunge right in *(hold chute behind back, go under and meet in middle)*,
Live for him *(reverse out and hold the chute taut in front of you again)*.
There's a fountain flowing *(ripple chute)*
Deep *(chute low and loose)* and wide *(chute high and taut)*.

When you have finished, relax on the chute together.

Reflections

'The life-giving fountain belongs to you, and your light gives light to each of us' (Psalm 36:9). How do we know that God's love is unfailing? What is it like to drink from a fountain? What is it like to drink from God's fountain?

Connections

This theme connects with:
• Scrubbed clean (see page 64)

Be still and know

Bible background

Psalm 46 (especially verse 10)

Theme

Be still, and know that I am God.

Activity summary

This is a reflective activity for use with a gentle worship song. Find the lyrics and tune for 'Be still and know' in *Complete Junior Praise* (22).

You will need:
• One chute

Parachute fun!

Ground the chute and ask all but four helpers to lie down on one half of the chute and relax quietly on it. Encourage them to breathe in and out deeply and steadily. The helpers slowly and gently cover and uncover the players lying down with the other half of the chute. Allow the chute to ripple and waft as you sing or listen to the song together. Stop, swap and start as necessary.

Reflections

Read parts of Psalm 46. How do we know that God is with us and looking after us even when things go wrong?

Connections

Use this activity as a blessing. Repeat Psalm 4:8 as you do so: 'I can lie down and sleep soundly because you, Lord, will keep me safe.'

Scrubbed clean

Bible background

Psalm 51

Theme

David asks God to forgive him.

Activity summary

This is a moderate-energy reflection combining two old favourites: 'Grandma's washing' and 'Washing machine'.

You will need:
• Paper confetti to be washing powder (optional)

Parachute fun!

Hold the chute mid-height in front of you, thumbs up. Learn chant A and 'toss' people into the tub (under the chute), small groups at a time. Those remaining around the chute spread themselves out evenly and recite chant B. Stop, swap and start until everyone is clean!

Chant A: Grandma's washing, Grandma's washing, rub, rub, rub *(shimmy chute from side to side)*.
Picked up [name of player and item of clothing, such as 'Sarah's purple top'] and threw it in the tub *(gently 'toss' player under the chute)*.

Chant B: Add the powder *(sprinkle paper confetti on the washing)*,
Turn it on *(click a finger but don't let go of chute)*,
Water in *(rustle the chute gently between your fingertips)*,
Rotate *(shake the chute while passing it clockwise between your hands)*,
Spin *(run the chute clockwise, holding it taut in your right hand)*,
Dry *(waft the chute gently)*,
Done *(call the 'washing' out)*.

Reflections

David wrote this prayer because he had done something wrong. He wanted God to forgive him and was so sorry that he wanted to change. Explore Psalm 51:1–11. The *MESSAGE* version of this passage is great, and the verses below are particularly appropriate.

Reproduced with permission from *Parachute Fun for Everyone* published by BRF 2011 (978 1 84101 702 0)
www.barnabasinchurches.org.uk

God, give grace! Huge in mercy—wipe out my bad record. Scrub away my guilt, soak out my sins in your laundry… and I'll come out clean, scrub me and I'll have a snow-white life… God, make a fresh start in me (vv. 1–2, 7, 10).

Connections

This theme connects with:

- Sing of God's love (see page 69)

Sea stills

Bible background

Psalm 69:34

Theme

Heaven and earth will praise our God, and so will the oceans and everything in them.

Activity summary

This set of activities contains those that are both energetic and reflective. You will play a few sea-themed games and work together to create sea creatures.

You will need:

- Upbeat worship music or sea sounds (for Nessie monster game)
- Things to make a simple obstacle course (for sea turtle game)
- Seaweed made from strips of bin bag stretched into bumpy shapes; coral made from colourful scarves or streamers; beanbag sea creatures or squishy balls with spikes (for rock pool game)
- Bubbles

Parachute fun!

Surfing

This game involves a high level of trust. The safest way to surf is to fold the chute into thirds. The surfer should stand in a surfing pose midway, facing forward. Two or three people pull carefully from the front. Make sure everyone knows the signal for 'stop'. Stop, swap and start as necessary.

Sharks

Hold the taut chute mid-height in front of you. Choose a 'shark' to go under the chute, one hand poking up like a fin, so that it can be seen moving on top.

The shark gently tweaks the knees of a 'swimmer', who screams, disappears under the chute and trades places with the shark. Continue to play until everyone has had a go. For extra fun, add 'coastguards' to circle the chute and save the 'swimmers', or freak weather conditions like 'tidal wave' *(one side of the chute sends a large wave to the other side)*, 'hurricane' *(run the chute clockwise)* or 'storm at sea' *(shake the chute vigorously)*.

Rock pool

Lay the chute out in a rock pool shape or pretend it is the sea. Add seaweed, beanbag creatures, coral and squishy balls. Ripple the chute gently to create lapping waves; shake it to increase the wind and waves. Take turns swimming or trying to avoid being caught in the seaweed. Blow bubbles together.

Giant crab

Crouch down and hold the chute taut under your chin. Move in a scuttling motion together.

Giant jellyfish

Loft the chute full of air; move it around and wobble it together.

Giant sea turtle

Hold the chute with both hands behind your back and bend over under it. Move the turtle together. For added fun, let the handles go so that the chute merely drapes over you. Set up an obstacle course and see if you can cover it without losing your 'shell'.

Nessie monster

Fold the chute lengthwise, twice. Hold it high above your heads. Bob up and down as you walk and sway your arms from side to side to make Nessie swim. Put on some worship music or sea sounds and move while it plays. Stop when the music stops.

Amoeba

Loft the chute, step in and bring it down behind you so that you are sitting on the edges; rock left and right to wobble it. Blow bubbles together inside.

Reflections

Memorise the verse together while you are all in the amoeba or sitting by the rock pool.

Connections

This theme connects with:
• God's creation (see page 22)

Sing of God's love

Bible background

Psalm 89:1–4

Theme

Our Lord, I will sing of your love for ever. Everyone yet to be born
will hear me praise your faithfulness (Psalm 89:1).

Activity summary

Participants will create their own worship response to a chosen
song, using a parachute and other props.

You will need:

- One chute (or two)
- Props: streamers, flags, ribbon balls, balloons
- Decorations: ribbons, bells, plastic pockets for artwork and so on
- Instruments

Choose a song to sing or play as accompaniment. Some suggestions
might be:

- I will sing of the mercies of the Lord for ever
  (www.my.homewithgod.com/heavenlymidis2/mercies.html)
- I could sing of your love for ever
  (www.delirious.org.uk/lyrics/songs/icouldsing.html)
- Praise him, praise him, all you little children (*Complete Junior
  Praise* 201)
- God is good (*Complete Junior Praise* 55)

Parachute fun!

Encourage participants to work together. Decorate the chute and use the props to create a worship routine to the chosen song. When the group has achieved this, use what they have created in worship and reflect together as below.

Reflections

Read Psalm 89:1–4 together. God promised David that someone from his family would always be king (2 Samuel 7:12–17). This psalm was written many years later by Ethan.

There was a problem. The king on the throne was not from David's family but was a Babylonian: King Nebuchadnezzar. Ethan was confused. Even though he couldn't explain it, he still believed that God was somehow doing what he had promised. He was right. Jesus is a king from David's family and he has always been on the throne for ever. God was keeping his promise even when it didn't seem as if he was.

Singing songs like this one teach us to trust God to keep his promises, even when we don't understand what is happening.

Connections

This theme connects with:
• Miriam sings a song (see page 52)

Wonderfully made

Bible background

Psalm 139:1–18, 23–24

Theme

We are wonderfully made by God. God knows everything about us and wants us to know him.

Activity summary

This reflection could be either reflective or energetic.

You will need:
• One chute

Parachute fun!

Ground the chute and lie restfully on top of it while the leader reads Psalm 139:1–18 and 23–24.

Stand up and hold the chute at mid-height, thumbs down. Practise the following activity several times until you can achieve it in a calm and prayerful manner. Choose a few people at a time to lie under the chute and enjoy the experience.

This is a call-and-response activity. The leader speaks the words in normal print below, and everyone responds together by doing the actions shown in italics.

Call and response

When I stand up *(stand up, chute to chin)*,
When I sit down *(sit down, chute to ground)*,
When I walk *(stand up, walk the chute around clockwise)*,
When I run *(run the chute around anti-clockwise)*,
In the heavens *(take one step in, loft the chute high)*,
Over the sea *(return chute to mid-height and ripple gently)*,
When I sleep *(tuck yourselves under the chute like a blanket)*,
In darkness *(loft the chute, step under, hold handles behind your back)*,
In light *(step out and hold chute mid-height)*,

Your hand is on me *(right hand holding the chute, left hand on the shoulder of the person on your left).*
You hold me *(group hug: move forward until you are hugging the person on your left with your left arm and holding the chute with your right hand).*
Your Spirit is with me *(move back, loft the chute and let it go).*

Reflections

How does this psalm make you feel about yourself, each other and God?

Connections

This theme connects with:
• God's creation (see page 22)

Come, praise the Lord

Bible background

Psalm 148

Theme

Every living thing is commanded to praise the Lord.

Activity summary

This is a reflective call-and-response activity. It is appropriate for all ages and abilities.

You will need:
• One chute

Parachute fun!

Hold the chute mid-height in both hands, thumbs up. The leader speaks the words in normal print below. Everyone responds together by speaking the words shown in italics as they loft and lower the chute.

Call and response

Day and night, dark and light; *come, praise the Lord alone*.
Highest heavens and angels above; *come, praise the Lord alone*.
Earth and sea, plants and trees; *come, praise the Lord alone*.
Sun, moon and stars, planets afar; *come, praise the Lord alone*.
Sea creatures and birds; *come, praise the Lord alone*.
Wild animals and tame; *come, praise the Lord alone*.
Everyone everywhere, young and old; *come, praise the Lord alone*.
All creation praise the name of the Lord; *praise his name alone*.

Reflections

Lay the chute out on grass and look up into the sky. Praise the Lord alone.

Connections

This theme connects with:
- God's creation (see page 22)
- The wonders of God (see page 59)
- Sea stills (see page 66)
- Sing of God's love (see page 69)

* * *

Wise friends

Bible background

Proverbs 12:26

Theme

The godly give good advice to their friends; the wicked lead them astray (Proverbs 12:26, NLT).

Activity summary

This is an energetic game involving percussion instruments and a chant.

You will need:
- Chant, as below
- Percussion instruments

Parachute fun!

Sit around the chute (swamp). Hold it taut under your chin with your legs stretched out underneath. Distribute instruments to help keep the beat. Practise the chant together: 'Gator, gator, in the swamp! Gator, gator, chomp, chomp, chomp!'

Choose an 'alligator' to crawl around under the chute, looking for a victim. When the chant has finished, the 'alligator' either drags a victim under the chute (beware bumped heads!) or tickles their toes. The victim then becomes an alligator. For added fun, choose a couple of 'wildlife rangers' to rescue those who are disappearing.

Reflections

Our friends can help us or drag us under. What kind of friends do you have? What kind of friend are you? How can we choose our friends carefully?

Connections

This theme connects with:
- Helping to heal (see page 87)

Gospel stories

The birth of Jesus

Bible background

Matthew 1:18; Luke 2:1–7

Theme

Jesus is born in a Bethlehem stable.

Activity summary

'The Virgin Mary had a baby boy' is a well-known Christmas carol. Find complete lyrics and tune in *Complete Junior Praise* (251). The actions below can also be adapted for use with 'Mary had a little baby' (*Complete Junior Praise* 164).

You will need:
• One chute
• Your own version of the story

Parachute fun!

Hold the chute mid-height, thumbs down. Count off in twos around the chute. Sing the song as follows:

Verse 1

The Virgin Mary had a baby boy *(x 3)*
And they say that his name was Jesus *(rock chute from side to side)*.

Chorus

He come from the glory *(loft the chute with your right hand)*,
He come from the glorious kingdom *(lower the chute again)*.
He come from the glory *(loft the chute with your left hand)*,
He come from the glorious kingdom *(lower the chute again)*.

O, yes, believer *('ones' loft the chute with both hands; 'twos' spin around on the spot),*
O, yes, believer *('twos' loft the chute with both hands; 'ones' spin around on the spot),*
He come from the glory *(all hold the chute and dance to the middle),*
He come from the glorious kingdom *(all dance out again).*

Verse 2

The angels sang when the baby was born *(x 3)*
And proclaimed him the Saviour Jesus.

Repeat Chorus.

Verse 3

The wise men saw where the baby was born *(x 3)*
And they saw that his name was Jesus.

Repeat Chorus.

Reflections

Tell the story as you think best for your group. Jan Dyer uses the colours of her chute to tell the life of Jesus as well as exploring the Christian life. See *100 Children's Club Activities* (Kingsway, 2001), pp. 219–221.

Connections

Small children love to rock their teddies as they sing 'Away in a manger' or 'Silent night'.

Temple tale

Bible background

Luke 2:40–52

Theme

Jesus is found teaching in the temple as a boy.

Activity summary

This is a moderate-energy role-play activity.

You will need:

- One or two chutes
- Beanbag chairs, carpet squares or pillows
- Story-related books, objects, music, worksheets or craft activities
- Your own version of the story

Parachute fun!

Before the session, create a 'temple' or sacred space by draping one chute over tall objects or suspending it from the ceiling. Leave one side of the chute open like a tent so that people can gather under it and spill out into the hall. You could use another chute for the floor. Provide this space with appropriate seating and story-related activities.

Make getting to the 'temple' an activity in itself. Pair up at the door and journey together around the room. Play a game of 'We're going to the temple' as follows:

The first pair starts the chant and adds an object: 'We're going to the temple and we're bringing a (Bible)'. The next pair chants, repeating the first object (Bible) and adding another (toothbrush). Play until everyone has added to the list. End when you arrive at the temple.

Tell a version of the story that is appropriate for your group and setting.

Reflections

Gather in groups and chat about some of the following questions. Encourage everyone to participate.

Why is it good to talk with others about God? Who can you talk to about God? How do you think Jesus got to understand so much? Have you ever had a misunderstanding with your parents? How is a misunderstanding different from a misdeed (wrongdoing)? How could this situation be avoided in the future? How does it feel when you have to choose between doing what God wants and doing what someone else wants?

Connections

Ask a church leader to come along and answer questions. Talk with the children about how important it was for Jesus to know the scriptures.

You could use this idea in a series over several weeks: Jesus in the stable, Jesus teaches in the temple, Jesus turns the tables, Jesus' last meal, Jesus in the tomb, Jesus rises from the dead.

You could also explore the idea of persecuted church, then and now. Create a tent by lofting the chute, bringing it down behind you and sitting on the inside edge. Someone stands in the centre to act as a tent pole. Pretend that you are having a secret meeting because you are not allowed to worship openly or own a Bible. Light the space with a non-flame light source. Talk and sing quietly, share all the Bible verses you know and pray for Christians who really have to meet like this.

* * *

Four fishermen

Bible background

Luke 5:1–11 (see also Matthew 4:18–22). There are complete lists of all the disciples in Matthew 10:1–4 and Luke 6:12–16.

Theme

Jesus chooses Peter, Andrew, James and John.

Activity summary

This is an energetic story starter and story combined, and includes a craft.

You will need:
- 22 card fish shapes with the story points below written on them
- Other fish shapes with nothing written on them

Parachute fun!

Place the numbered fish story cards and several blank fish cards on the chute (net). Hold it mid-height and ripple it gently. A leader does a silly walk around the chute and taps a follower on the shoulder. The follower lays down their 'net' and follows the leader, repeating the silly walk. The leader continues to choose followers randomly until everyone has laid down their 'net' and is following. Change the style of the silly walk several times throughout.

When you have finished, ask everyone to find a fish story card (double up if necessary) and sit around the chute. Read the story in order. Write your own names on the blank fish and pray for one another as you return them to the 'net'.

1. One day, Jesus was teaching by the sea.
2. A crowd of fishermen, traders and people from nearby towns were listening.
3. Jesus saw two fishing boats on the shore nearby.
4. James and his brother John were mending their nets.
5. Simon Peter and his brother Andrew were also mending their nets.
6. Jesus asked Simon Peter to take him out a little way in their boat.
7. When Jesus finished teaching the crowds, they began to leave.
8. Jesus told Simon Peter, 'Row out deeper and put your nets in to catch some fish.'
9. Simon Peter and Andrew were tired from fishing all night.
10. 'Teacher, we've worked hard and haven't caught a thing,' said Simon Peter. 'But we'll try.'
11. It was an amazing catch—so amazing that the nets began to rip apart.
12. They waved to their partners, James and John, for help.
13. James and John rowed out in their boat and helped to bring the fish ashore.
14. Both boats were so full that they began to sink.
15. The fishermen were in awe. They knew there was something special about Jesus.
16. Simon Peter fell to his knees before Jesus.
17. 'Don't be afraid!' said Jesus. 'Follow me and I will teach you how to fish for people.'
18. They all pulled their boats on to the shore.
19. They left their nets and everything else and went with Jesus.
20. They followed God's way and learned how to bring people to God.
21. In time, Jesus chose eight other people especially to help him tell others about God.
22. They were Matthew, Thomas, Philip, Bartholomew, Thaddaeus, James, Simon and Judas Iscariot.

Reflections

Do you think it was silly for the disciples to leave everything and follow Jesus? What do you think they had to leave behind? What was so special about Jesus that they wanted to follow him?

Jesus needed people to show other people how to follow God's way. How did his disciples do this? How do we do this today? The people Jesus chose were quite ordinary. Why is it good to have different kinds of people to tell people about God? Jesus often sent his disciples to work in pairs. Remind everyone that we are a part of the great catch of 'fish' (believers) that Jesus promised to his early disciples.

Connections

Use story cards and fish to create a wall display.

This theme connects with:
- Fishing for followers (see below)
- Fishing all night (see page 99)
- Breakfast with Jesus (see page 100)

Fishing for followers

Bible background

Matthew 4:19

Theme

Jesus said, 'Come, follow me and I will show you how to fish for people!' (NLT)

Activity summary

This is an energetic activity sung to the tune of 'Row, row, row your boat'. It has been adapted from *100s of Songs, Games and More* (Cook Communications, 2003).

You will need:
• One chute

Parachute fun!

Divide the group into 'fishermen' and 'fish'. The fishermen pretend the chute is a net and catch the fish. Sing the song as follows, to the tune of 'Row, row, row your boat':

Get, get, get your net *(pick up the chute like a net),*
Throw it in the sea *(pretend to toss the chute into the sea).*
Pull it in, all full of fish *(fish jump on to the net),*
Then come and follow me *(fishermen pull fish around on the chute).*

Reflections

Learn Matthew 4:19 together.

Connections

You could also begin this activity by singing 'Row, row, row your boat'. Everyone sits around the chute with legs underneath and holds the chute. One half rows against the other half as you would with a partner. Sing it with different voices or at different speeds for more fun.

This theme connects with:
• Four fishermen (see page 82)
• Into all the world (see page 97)
• Fishing all night (see page 99)
• Breakfast with Jesus (see page 100)

Thanks for everything

Bible background

Matthew 6:25–34; 1 Thessalonians 5:16–18

Theme

Don't be anxious: God takes care of everything. Birds that sing and food to eat—everything.

Activity summary

This is a reflective prayer to a popular musical grace.

You will need:
- One chute
- Ribbons to attach to the handles of the chute
- The grace 'Thank you for the world so sweet'

Parachute fun!

The chute will become a merry-go-round. Tie ribbons to the handles, lay it on the ground and stand around it. Choose someone to sit and ride in the centre. Hold the chute in your right hand and face out to the left. Your left arm is extended to flap like a bird's wing. The chute should be taut enough to keep the centre person on the ground.

Sing the grace below as you rotate the chute clockwise. Move your bodies up and down. Swap hands, change direction and sing it again. When you have finished, put the chute back on the ground and sit down.

Thank you for the world so sweet.
Thank you for the food we eat.
Thank you for the birds that sing.
Thank you, Lord, for everything.

Reflections

Explore Matthew 6:25–34 together. Why doesn't God want us to worry?

1 Thessalonians 5:16–18 says, 'Always be joyful and never stop praying. Whatever happens, keep thanking God because of Jesus Christ. This is what God wants you to do.' Discuss how choosing to be thankful makes life much sweeter, even when there are difficult times.

Connections

This theme connects with:

- God's creation (see page 22)
- Feeding five thousand (see page 89)

Helping to heal

Bible background

Mark 2:1–12 (see also Matthew 9:1–8; Luke 5:17–26)

Activity summary

This is a trust exercise and story starter. It should only be done with a person if there is appropriate supervision and established trust within the group.

You will need:
- One chute
- Your own version of the story

Parachute fun!

Start with the chute on the ground and everyone standing around it. Give each person a disability, such as a blindfold for their eyes or a sling for their arms, or have them hop on one foot. Give some people ear plugs for hearing impairment. Ask some of them to pretend they have a bad sneeze or a cough. Play a simple chute game and see how difficult it is to play. Now 'heal' some people and play again. Was it easier when friends could help? When you have finished, lay the chute back on the ground.

After the activity, open the chute and make a house. Loft the chute, pull it down behind you and sit on the edges. Tell a simple version of the story.

Reflections

We can thank God when we are healthy, but not everyone is always healthy. Only God can do miracles, but we can do our part to help. Do we know someone who needs healing? How can we help to make things better? How can love help to heal?

Connections

Talk about how hands can help. You could also fold the chute into a rectangular mat, then choose someone to lie still on it and four 'friends' to walk with it and lift it over an obstacle. Stop, start and swap as necessary.

This theme connects with:
- Decorate a chute (see page 20)
- Wise friends (see page 74)
- Lazarus lives (see page 90)

Feeding five thousand

Bible background

John 6:1–14 (see also Matthew 14:13–21; Mark 6:30–44; Luke 9:10–17)

Theme

Jesus feeds 5000 people with five loaves and two fish.

Activity summary

This is an energetic call-and-response story starter, followed by a picnic.

You will need:
- Fish-shaped sandwiches, snacks and juice
- Percussion instruments (optional)
- Your own version of the story

Parachute fun!

Give the instruments to those who might find it otherwise difficult to participate. Hold the chute taut, mid-height in your right hand. Walk clockwise as you call and respond:

Leader: We're going to the mountain.
Echo: We're going to the mountain.
Leader: We're going to see Jesus.
Echo: We're going to see Jesus.
Leader: How will we get there?
Echo: How will we get there?

Leader: Let's hop *(hop for a bit, then return to a walk for the chant)*… skip, run, march, gallop, jump, silly walk, raise our hands, touch our noses, stick out our tongues, give a cheer *(and so on)*.

Leader: *(Last time)* We're there! *(Collapse on to chute together.)*

Now make a mountain. Loft the chute, snap it down quickly in front of you and kneel on the edge. Trap as much air as possible inside. Allow one or two people to climb the mountain at a time. When the chute is deflated, invite the children to rest on it.

Reflections

Have your own picnic as you tell the story. Chat about the boy who gave what he had to Jesus. What do you have to give? What is one way in which you can share what you have with others? How can we help those who are hungry in our world today? Have you ever known something unexpected to happen? If you could ask Jesus to do one thing, what would it be?

Connections

This theme connects with:
• Thanks for everything (see page 86)

Lazarus lives

Bible background

John 11:1–45

Theme

Jesus makes Lazarus live again.

You will need:
- One chute
- Your own version of the story

Activity summary

This is a reflective story starter, which should be handled sensitively with a group you know well.

Parachute fun!

Ground the chute and stand around it. Choose a 'Lazarus' to lie down in the centre, face up, with arms at the sides and eyes closed. Everyone else should now hold the chute with their right hand. Walk quietly clockwise. The circle will gradually decrease and 'Lazarus' will be wrapped up. Reverse at a quicker pace to reveal a risen 'Lazarus'. Make sure that 'Lazarus' feels comfortable and is not wrapped too tightly.

Players can lie down under the chute as you tell the story.

Reflections

Think about the different characters in the story and what they might be feeling as the story unfolds. You could also think about Jesus rising from the dead.

Connections

This theme connects with:
- Helping to heal (see page 87)
- Rolled away (see page 113)

One way

Bible background

John 14:6

Theme

Jesus talks to his disciples about heaven.

Activity summary

This is a reflective activity that involves making a maze.

You will need:
- One or more chutes
- A big ball of string or wool
- A prize, and John 14:6 written out on card
- Reflective worship music

Parachute fun!

Create a maze together on the chute(s) using one continuous piece of string. Include lots of twists and turns and a prize at the end of the string. Participants must walk on top of the string as if it were a tightrope to get their prize.

Reflections

Jesus said, 'I am the way, the truth, and the life! Without me, no one can go to the Father' (John 14:6). What do you think this verse means?

Connections

This theme connects with:
- Adam's apple (see page 27)
- I am (see below)

I am

Bible background

I am / the one who / raises the dead to life! / Everyone / who has faith in me / will live / even if they die. / John 11:25

Theme

Seven 'I am' statements:

- I am the bread that gives life! (John 6:35, 48)
- I am the light for the world! (John 8:12; 9:5)
- I am the gate (John 10:7, 9)
- I am the good shepherd (John 10:11, 14)
- I am the one who raises the dead to life! (John 11:25)
- I am the way, the truth, and the life! (John 14:6)
- I am the true vine (John 15:1, 5)

Activity summary

This is a moderate-energy memory box jumble and reflection. You will memorise John 11:25 and explore six other 'I am' statements.

You will need:
- Eight large empty tissue boxes wrapped in light paper
- One of each of the above statements and its reference, written or typed on card

- One light, unbreakable item to wrap inside each of seven of the boxes: bread, torch, a gate latch, sheep, cross, map and vine
- Laminated copies of John 11:25, one per person, to wrap in the remaining box

Write part of John 11:25 on each of seven of the boxes, using a permanent marker. Make sure to include the verse reference on the eighth box on its own. Place an object, along with its 'I am' statement, in each of the seven boxes and tape them closed. Place the laminated copies of John 11:25 in the eighth box and tape it closed.

Parachute fun!

Stand around the chute. Put the memory boxes in order in the centre of the chute and read John 11:25 together. Shake the chute to scramble the boxes, and work together to put the verse back in order. Do this several times.

Reflections

When you have finished playing, relax on the chute and unwrap the seven 'I am' boxes one at a time, chatting as you go. To finish, open the eighth box and give everyone a laminated copy of John 11:25 to take home.

Connections

This activity also works well as a way of learning the order of the books in the Bible book. You can also put props to tell a story in the boxes or role-play ideas.

This theme connects with:
- Adam's apple (see page 27)
- One way (see page 92)

✱ ✱ ✱

Mary's gift

Bible background

John 12:1–8

Theme

Mary uses an expensive bottle of perfume to wash Jesus' feet.

Activity summary

This is a reflective story.

You will need:
- Several different kinds of wrapping paper
- Sample perfume or lotion packets
- Numbered story cards (1–12)
- Reflective worship music

Wrap a pass-the-parcel with a different story card and sample perfume packet in each layer. Story card 1 will be the first to be unwrapped and story card 12 will be the last.

Parachute fun!

Hold the chute mid-height, thumbs up. Bounce the parcel up and down while the music plays. When the music stops, the leader calls out a name. Move the parcel toward the chosen person by using the chute. The person opens a layer of the parcel, reads a bit of the story and keeps the perfume packet until needed. Play again until all the cards have been read. Give extra perfume packets to those who did not get a turn opening the parcel.

1. One night, Jesus stopped to visit his friends: Mary, Martha and Lazarus.
2. They were so glad to see Jesus and his disciples that they invited them in.
3. Mary and Martha prepared a special dinner.
4. Everyone was enjoying each other's company around the table. They were still amazed that Lazarus was alive.
5. Mary brought in a jar of expensive perfume, usually used to welcome guests or prepare bodies for burial.
6. Everyone wondered what Mary was going to do.
7. Mary knelt in front of Jesus and poured the perfume on his feet. Then she wiped his feet with her long hair.
8. The room smelled lovely and sweet.
9. Judas was cross. He said that he'd wanted to sell the perfume and give the money to those in need.
10. This was a lie. Judas really wanted to keep the money for himself, as he often did.
11. Jesus defended Mary. He knew that he would die soon and that what Mary had done was really special.
12. 'Leave her alone,' said Jesus. 'This perfume was intended for my burial. You will not always have me here.'

Reflections

When you have finished, sit on the chute together. Summarise the story and chat about the piece of worship music you have heard. Put the lotion or perfume on each other's hands or feet.

Connections

You could also use this activity to explore salvation as a free gift, chanting Ephesians 2:8–9 as you move the parcel.

Gospel stories

* * *

Into all the world

Bible background

Matthew 28:19–20 (see also Mark 16:15–18; Luke 24:46–51)

Theme

Jesus tells his disciples to go and make disciples.

Activity summary

This is a reflective theme activity. The chute will be used as a large living compass with the help of a ball of string. It can be adapted for group size: complete (16 players or more), medium (eight players or more) or simple for younger children. It is better to use more than one chute if numbers allow.

You will need:
- One or more chutes
- A large ball of string
- Compass points written on cards
- A pair of scissors

Complete (16)

N NNE NE ENE E ESE SE SSE S SSW SW WSW W WNW NW NNW

Medium (8)

N NE E SE S SW W NW

Simple (4)

N S E W

Parachute fun!

Place the compass point cards around the outside of the chute. Choose a North and allow players to lay the other cards, if you like. Ask one player to sit at each compass point, ready for play, while everyone else fills in the gaps.

Give one ball of string to the player at North. Ask them to hold the end of the string firmly in one hand and the ball in the other. Explain that different compass points will be called. The ball will be tossed from player to player. Each time the ball is thrown, the player catching it will take hold of the string, pull it taut, hold on to it and toss the ball to the next compass point called.

An easy star pattern will work with the medium compass: N SW NE S NW SE N (E and W are not used). When the ball returns to North, everyone stands up together and admires the star shape they have created. Sit down again and undo the compass by calling the points in reverse. Each player winds the string back on to the ball as you go. Have a pair of scissors handy to clip the string and start again if you get in a muddle. Change the players at the compass points so that everyone can have a go.

Once you have achieved a star, players can call (and use all) the compass points at random. Stand up occasionally to see what patterns emerge.

Reflections

Jesus said, 'Go to the people of all nations and make them my disciples... I will be with you always, even until the end of the world' (Matthew 28:19–20).

Talk about the Christians you know and how many there are in the world. There are so many because the first believers did what Jesus asked. Thank God for the people who are helping you to follow Jesus. How can we go everywhere and do the same?

Connections

This theme connects with:
• Four fishermen (see page 82)

You could also explore Psalm 103:12.

Fishing all night

Bible background

John 21:1–14

Theme

Jesus has died, and his disciples go fishing.

Activity summary

This is a reflective story starter that requires coordination and teamwork to be achieved in a flowing way. The chutes represent nets and the motion is like casting and gathering.

You will need:
• Two chutes
• Sea sounds or music

Parachute fun!

Begin with both groups standing beside each other, holding their chutes in both hands. Leave a two-section gap on opposite sides where no one is holding the chute (this will be used to create a lane). Group one will loft their chute while group two passes underneath and out the other side. Group two will then loft their chute while group one passes underneath. Continue this alternating over-and-under pattern for a set distance or time.

When you have finished, ask everyone to sit around the outside edge of one of the chutes. Pretend it is the sea and you are all sitting on the beach. Ripple the chute gently. Take your shoes off and dip your toes in. Tell the story of 'Breakfast with Jesus' (see below).

Reflections

What do we do when we are discouraged or sad?

Connections

This theme connects with:
- Sea stills (see page 66)
- Four fishermen (see page 82)
- Thanks for everything (see page 86)
- Breakfast with Jesus (see below)

Breakfast with Jesus

Bible background

John 21:1–14

Theme

The risen Jesus makes breakfast for the discouraged disciples.

Activity summary

This is a reflective role-play story that involves a craft, game and food.

You will need:

- 153 large double-sided fish in different colours, each with a paperclip attached (your group could make these before play)
- A verse of your choice written on each fish
- Snacks with colour-coded dots to correspond with the colours of the fish
- Several fishing poles (one between two or three) made from dowels
- String and a magnet for a hook
- Bibles

Parachute fun!

Choose people to act out the characters in the story as you tell it.

Story

One night, after Jesus had died and come back to life, some of his friends were fishing from a boat in the sea (*disciples in the centre of the chute, pretending to toss and gather their nets*). It was hard work throwing their nets out and gathering them back in. They had been doing it all night and hadn't caught a single fish.

Early in the morning, they saw a man standing on the shore nearby. 'Did you catch anything?' he asked. (*Jesus stands at the outside edge of the chute and asks the question.*)

'No!' they called back. You could tell they were tired. (*Disciples answer wearily.*)

'Lower your net to the right side of the boat,' called the man, 'and you will find some!' (*Jesus repeats.*)

Jesus' friends threw the net back into the water one more time—and an amazing thing happened! The net was full of fish, so heavy that they couldn't even pull it up into the boat. (*Leader pours the fish around the disciples.*)

Reproduced with permission from *Parachute Fun for Everyone* published by BRF 2011 (978 1 84101 702 0)
www.barnabasinchurches.org.uk

Now John had seen this happen once before, and it was John who first recognised the man on the shore. 'It's the Lord!' he said to Peter. *(John repeats.)*

Peter couldn't wait. He jumped into the water and began to swim. The others followed him, dragging the heavy net behind the boat. *(Peter jumps into the water while the others gather the fish.)*

By the time everyone got to the beach, Jesus was already cooking some fish over a fire. There was also some bread and they were all really hungry. 'Bring me some of your fish,' he said.

Peter dragged the net ashore. There were 153 large fish in it and the net didn't even burst. 'Come and have breakfast,' Jesus said, so they did. *(Jesus pretends to cook fish and disciples pretend to eat it.)*

Show everyone how many there are! Go fishing for your snack. Put the fish on the chute and use the magnets on the end of the fishing poles. Before collecting colour-coded snacks from the table, look up your chosen verse and read it out loud.

Reflections

Chat about your chosen verses. How do you know that Jesus is with you even when you can't see him?

Connections

This theme connects with:
- Four fishermen (see page 82)
- Fishing for followers (see page 84)
- Thanks for everything (see page 86)
- Fishing all night (see page 99)

Getting together

Bible background

Matthew 18:19–20

Theme

'Whenever two or three of you come together in my name, I am there with you' (Matthew 18:20).

Activity summary

This is a reflective prayer activity and memory verse based on an old grace.

You will need:
• One chute

Parachute fun!

Stand around the chute and hold it mid-height. Use the following chant:

When we gather together (*hold chute with right hand, move clockwise*)
To worship the Lord (*loft chute high*),
Jesus is with us (*hold chute with left hand and move anti-clockwise*),
Our risen Lord (*down on one knee, chute high*).

Reflections

What does it mean to agree on something in prayer? Will we always get what we pray for? Why or why not? How do we know that Jesus is with us when we gather together?

Connections

This theme connects with:

• Rolled away (see page 113)

The needle's eye

Bible background

Matthew 19:16–30 (see also Mark 10:17–31; Luke 18:18–30)

Theme

A rich ruler keeps the commandments and his money but loses his soul.

Activity summary

This is an energetic story starter and ball game.

You will need:

• Three medium or large foam balls

Parachute fun!

Ground the chute. Stand around the edge, legs apart, feet touching (each forming the 'eye of a needle'). Three players stand back to back in the centre of the chute, each holding a ball (camel hump).

Each must get their 'camel hump' through the 'eye of a needle'. Players around the edge may try to prevent this, using their arms and hands but not their feet. If a ball goes through, the players trade places.

Reflections

'It's easier for a camel to go through the eye of a needle than for a rich person to get into God's kingdom' (Matthew 19:24). Why? What does Jesus mean?

Connections

This theme connects with:
• Ten targets (see page 55)

Last and first

Bible background

Mark 9:33–37 (see also Luke 9:46–48)

Theme

Jesus settles an argument about who will be the greatest in his kingdom.

Activity summary

These moderate-energy theme games require teamwork. They represent the topsy-turvy nature of Jesus' teaching.

You will need:
• One chute

Parachute fun!

Overhead swing

Grasp the edge of the chute with a crossover grip (right hand over left, thumbs down). Swing the chute over your heads on the count of three while turning your bodies to the right. Now touch your toes with the edge of the chute. You will be on the inside of the chute. Do this as smoothly as possible and reverse to get out.

Inside out

Grasp the chute and hold it mid-height in front of you. Stretch out your hands so that they touch the hands of the players next to you. You must now work together to turn the chute inside out without letting go.

Reflections

What did Jesus mean when he said, 'If you want the place of honour, you must become a slave and serve others' (Mark 9:35)?

Connections

You could use this activity to talk about teamwork or repentance.

Widow's pennies

Bible background

Luke 21:1–4 (see also Mark 12:41–44)

Theme

Jesus sees some rich people give just a little of their wealth, and a woman who has very little give everything she has.

Activity summary

This is an energetic story starter followed by a reflection.

You will need:
- A penny for everyone
- A container

Parachute fun!

This is a team relay. Everyone is given a coin and stands around the chute. Players on opposite sides run against one another. Non-runners loft and lower the chute throughout.

Put the container in the middle under the chute. Choose a pair to start. They must run clockwise around the chute and through the space left by their opponent, put their penny in the container, return to their space and tag the next person to go. The winning team is the one to get all of their pennies in the container first. When you have finished, gather everyone on to the chute.

Reflections

One day, Jesus looked up and saw some rich people tossing their gifts into the offering box at the temple. He also saw a widow who had very little, putting in only two pennies. Jesus said that the woman had actually given more because she gave everything she had and not just what she had to spare.

Jesus teaches us that it is more important to give of ourselves than it is to give simply from our wealth.

Give each child a coin. Play some worshipful music and take a special collection. Think about all kinds of giving: financial, praying, helping others, time and so on.

Connections

You could make coin rubbings and use these in the relay instead of real coins. How many pennies stay in the container after the wafting of the chute?

'When you do good deeds, don't try to show off. If you do, you won't get a reward from your Father in heaven' (Matthew 6:1).

Well watered

Bible background

John 4:3–42; 7:37–38

Theme

Jesus promises living water: 'No one who drinks the water I give will ever be thirsty again' (John 4:14).

Activity summary

This is an energetic theme game involving water balloons or wet sponges. It must be played outside.

You will need:
• Water balloons or wet sponges (the more, the better)

Parachute fun!

You will need lots of outdoor space. The chute will lie flat and act as a target for the water balloons or wet sponges. How you turn your chute into a target will depend on the type of chute you have.

If your chute is already ringed or dartboard-like in design, you will assign each section from the outer edge to the centre a points value. For example, landing in the outermost ring might be worth 20, the middle ring 30 and the centre 50. Landing on a ring divider itself might double the points in the section hit. If your chute is divided like a pie chart, you may want to use ropes to create ringed sections as above, or assign each wedge or colour a points value.

You may also prefer to use laminated shapes instead: circles might be worth 20, triangles 15 and squares 50. Points could be doubled if the team manages to hit all the shapes.

To play, divide your group into smaller teams. Each team should stand in a single line, spaced equally and at a challenging distance around the outside edge of the chute. The first person in each team takes a turn and then goes to the back of their line. Play for a set number of turns per person or for a set amount of time. For more control, play one person at a time. Remind everyone of safety.

Reflections

Talk about the many uses for water and why it is so important for our survival. Tell the story of the woman Jesus met at the well.

'If you are thirsty, come to me and drink! Have faith in me, and you will have life-giving water flowing from deep inside you, just as the Scriptures say' (John 7:37–38). In what way is Jesus life-giving water?

Connections

You could use this activity with any baptism or sea story. It is also fun to try this activity with Frisbees, beanbags, balls, pennies and so on. You can also add bins or buckets for participants to throw things into.

God's not dead

Bible background

John 4:24

Theme

'God is Spirit, and those who worship God must be led by the Spirit to worship him according to the truth.'

Activity summary

'God's not dead' is a traditional energetic action song which can also be chanted. Find lyrics, tune and a rap version at www. freekidsmusic.com/mps1/RonnieCaldwell_GodsNotDead.mp3.

You will need:

- One chute
- Percussion instruments (optional)

Parachute fun!

Hold the chute mid-height in both hands, thumbs up. Players around one half of the chute are group 1. Players around the other half are group 2. Choose percussionists to keep the beat (optional). Sing the song as follows:

Chorus

Group 1: God's not dead (*flick a quick wave from their side of the chute to the other*)

Group 2: No! (*flick a quick wave back*)

Everyone: He is alive! *(raise the chute up and snap it back to mid-height)*

Repeat Chorus three times.

Verse

All: I feel him in my hands *(shake the chute twice)*.

All: I feel him in my feet *(stamp feet twice)*.

All: I feel him in my heart *(turn around once, switching hands so as not to let go of the chute)*.

All: I feel him in my soul *(step forward and shimmy, step back)*.

All: I feel him all over me *(loft the chute high in both hands)*.

All: Raise your hands up to the roof and show the world you're living proof *(sway and rap together twice with chute held high)*

Repeat Chorus.

Last time: After 'I feel him in my soul' the leader chants: 'Feel him in my hands, feet, heart and head. I say, "God's not…" and you say' *(participants shout back)* 'DEAD'.

All: I feel him all over me *(loft the chute, step in and let the chute fall around you)*.

Reflections

How do we know that God is alive? What does it mean to say that God is Spirit?

Connections

This theme connects with:
- Ten targets (see page 55)
- Mary's gift (see page 95)
- Rolled away (see page 113)

A full life

Bible background

John 10:10

Theme

'I came so that everyone would have life, and have it fully.'

Activity summary

This jigsaw activity can be either energetic or reflective.

You will need:
• Two jigsaw puzzles with large pieces

Parachute fun!

Stand around the chute and count off by twos. Scramble the puzzles together using the chute. On the signal, each team works to separate their jigsaw from the other one and put it together. Take your time for a more reflective activity; use a timer for a more energetic activity.

Reflections

What does it mean to say that Jesus wants to make us whole?

Connections

You could also make your own paper jigsaws to any theme you choose.

This theme connects with:
• Adam's apple (see page 27)

Rolled away

Bible background

Matthew 28:1–10 (see also Mark 16:1–8; Luke 24:1–12; John 20:1–10)

Theme

'Suddenly a strong earthquake struck, and the Lord's angel came down from heaven. He rolled away the stone and sat on it' (Matthew 28:2).

Activity summary

This activity is based on roller ball and is sung to the gospel spiritual 'The angel rolled the stone away'. There are several versions of it. Find the tune at www.concordiarecordings.com/Merchant2/media/3723-17.mp3. Find sheet music and an alternative version at www.wlym.com/~oakland/docs/SpiritualHairston.pdf. It can be either reflective or energetic.

You will need:
• A huge lightweight ball (the bigger, the better)
• Your own version of the story

Parachute fun!

Start from a standing or kneeling position. Hold the chute taut in both hands, thumbs up. Place the ball in the centre of the chute.

During the verses, create a tremor: keep the chute taut and shimmy it quickly from side to side. The ball should move but remain on the chute.

During the chorus, roll the stone away. Roll the ball around the chute on large and gentle waves *or* roll it around on one continuous wave. Try to keep it on the chute.

Chorus (roller ball):

The angel rolled the stone away,
The angel rolled the stone away,
It was early Easter Sunday morning,
The angel rolled the stone away.

Verses (tremor):

Mary came a'running, about the break of day,
Looking for Lord Jesus, the stone was rolled away. *(Chorus)*

I'm looking for my Saviour, tell me where he lay,
High up on the mountain, the stone was rolled away. *(Chorus)*

The soldiers were aplenty, standing by the door,
But they could not hinder, the stone was rolled away. *(Chorus)*

Old Pilate and his wise men didn't know what to say,
The miracle was on them, the stone was rolled away. *(Chorus)*

Reflections

Tell the resurrection story as you think best for your group.

Connections

You can also use this activity with the song 'He's got the whole world in his hand'. Talk about our responsibility in taking care of the world.

If you have a giant ball, you could try ball balancing. A leader (or two) holds the ball steady between his or her knees while a participant is invited to climb on to the ball and sit on top of it. Once the participant is balanced, the leader(s) carefully move slightly away but remain ready to catch the participant if he or she begins to topple. This can also be attempted standing if the ball is big and sturdy enough and the participant is confident. Talk about what the early witnesses saw when they got to the tomb.

This theme connects with:
- Sing of God's love (see page 69)
- Lazarus lives (see page 90)
- Getting together (see page 103)

Categories index

Energetic

Moderate energy

Reflective

Art and crafts

Ball games

Call-and-response and chants

Memory verses

Music and instruments

Props and objects

Reflections and prayers

Role play

Games

Songs

Story starters

Stories

Multiple chutes

Please note: all activities may be done with one chute but those below may be more effective with two or more.

Bible index

Old Testament

New Testament

Resources

For playchute-related books and booklets:

Dyason, Duncan: www.woodlands-junior.kent.sch.uk/parachute.html

Mosley, Jenny and Sonnet, Helen, *Making Waves* (LDA, 2002)

Pryor, Dinah, *Don't Forget the Parachute: Environmental Games to Save our Planet* (SeamStress)

SeamStress Ltd, *Playchute Games 1, 2 and 3* (SeamStress, 1995)

SeamStress Ltd, *Playchutes in Christian Teaching* (SeamStress, 1999)

SeamStress Ltd, *Playchute Games for Early Years* (SeamStress, 2006)

Wilmes, Liz and Dick, *Parachute Play* (Building Blocks, 2000)

For playchutes, accessories and Octaband™:

www.octaband.com/products.htm (US-based)

www.playchutes.com (SeamStress Ltd: UK-based)

www.playparachutes.com/copa.html (US-based)

www.tts-group.co.uk (educational website: UK-based)

For crafts, food and other games:

www.daniellesplace.com/index.html (US based)

Dyer, Jan, *100 Children's Club Activities* (Kingsway, 2001)

Klein, Diane (et al.), *Strategies for Including Children with Special Needs in Early Childhood Settings* (Delmar, 2001), pp. 171–174

Pinchbeck, Lesley, *Theme Games* (Scripture Union, 1993)

Schmidt, Doug (ed.), *100s of Songs, Games and More* (Cook Communications, 2003)

About
brf:

BRF is a registered charity and also a limited company, and has been in existence since 1922. Through all that we do—producing resources, providing training, working face-to-face with adults and children, and via the web—we work to resource individuals and church communities in their Christian discipleship through the Bible, prayer and worship.

Our Barnabas children's team works with primary schools and churches to help children under 11, and the adults who work with them, to explore Christianity creatively and to bring the Bible alive.

To find out more about BRF and its core activities and ministries, visit:

www.brf.org.uk
www.brfonline.org.uk
www.barnabasinschools.org.uk
www.barnabasinchurches.org.uk
www.messychurch.org.uk
www.foundations21.org.uk

If you have any questions about BI
and our work, please email us

enquiries@brf.org.ul

enter